Jekyll ﹙

Gary McNair,
novel by Rober

T0228724

methuen | drama

LONDON • NEW YORK • OXFORD • NEW DELHI • SYDNEY

METHUEN DRAMA
Bloomsbury Publishing Plc
50 Bedford Square, London, WC1B 3DP, UK
1385 Broadway, New York, NY 10018, USA
29 Earlsfort Terrace, Dublin 2, Ireland

BLOOMSBURY, METHUEN DRAMA and the Methuen
Drama logo are trademarks of Bloomsbury Publishing Plc

First published in Great Britain 2024

A catalogue record for this book is available from the British Library.

A catalog record for this book is available from the Library of Congress.

ISBN: PB: 978-1-3504-7524-3
ePDF: 978-1-3504-7525-0
eBook: 978-1-3504-7526-7

Series: Modern Plays

Typeset by Mark Heslington Ltd, Scarborough, North Yorkshire

To find out more about our authors and books visit
www.bloomsbury.com and sign up for our newsletters.

Acknowledgements

With thanks to

Paul Stacey, Steph Weller, Nick Thompson and all at
Reading Rep
David Greig, Jackie Crichton, Hannah Roberts and all at
The Lyceum
Emily Hickman, Seán Butler and all at the Agency
Jamie Scott Gordon
Kieran Hurley
Paul Downie
Christie O'Carroll
Katy McNair

And special thanks to

Audrey Brisson for her incredible performance in this
show's first iteration. Audrey, thank you for your generosity,
your exploration, imagination, dedication, warmth, and
boundless talent. You will forever run through the life blood
of this show. Merci.

Writer's Note

When Reading Rep Theatre asked me to create a new version of *Jekyll and Hyde*, I jumped at the chance. I thought the fact that they wanted a Scottish writer to take on the task was great, more so that they thought that writer should be me. I loved taking the challenge of getting under the surface of this old story, famous for a plot twist that everyone already knows and trying to make it relevant for today.

I was extremely lucky that they assembled such a wonderful team lead by director Michael Fentiman. I was quite blown away by the haunting and mesmeric production they created, and I'm absolutely thrilled that The Lyceum have taken it on to present it here in Scotland.

It's a real honour to be presenting a show on The Lyceum stage for the first time. I made my first visit to The Lyceum when I was seventeen and prepping for my drama school audition. I fell in love with it instantly – yes, it was grand and beautiful and there was a real majesty to it but I loved the fact that it somehow retained an intimacy that made the space cosy and inviting and made the work feel very immediate. I left that night not only full of ideas for my audition but also with the thought 'Oh I tell you what, I'd love to put a show on in there one day'. The fact that, twenty years on, that day is here feels very special indeed.

What's more, something that made as big an impression on me that night as the venue was the performance from none other than Forbes Masson. I was a huge fan of his comedy work from TV (my VHS of *The High Life* was just about worn through) so I was very excited and surprised to see him walk out on to the stage in this 'serious play' (being a teenager who didn't read the programme, and this being before we had internet, I didn't know he was in it) and I was blown away by his presence on stage. His command of the space really stayed with me. So, the fact that Forbes is performing the role of Utterson makes this Lyceum debut all the more special.

Thank you for picking up a copy of this play, it means a great deal. I am always thrilled when my plays are published and more so at the idea of someone sitting down to read them. I hope you enjoy it.

Jekyll and Hyde

For Katy, Rosa and Leo

List of Characters

Utterson
Enfield
Lanyon
Jekyll
Poole
Witness
Copper

Prologue

A chair sits on a blank stage.

Behind it, a door.

Utterson *enters. Sits.*

A silence.

Utterson   Before we begin I'd like to say something.
I'm not the good guy in this story.
I'm not the villain!
No, that role is clearly filled.
And I'm not saying you wont like me. My charm. My
charisma.
You will, at times throughout, be taken in by me.
You will. You'll like me.
I'm likeable.
But I'm not the good guy. I think it's important to say that,
right here, right now, before we start, because I will have a
tendency throughout, as I think we all do, to present myself
as the hero. The good guy.

That I am not.

Right. OK, with that said.

This starts with a door.

A grotesque door in a grotesque lane, grotesquely tucked
away behind the more presentable quarters of London
where you and your presentable friends might gather.

Now, appearances don't usually matter that much to me.
Yes, sure, I take care of myself and I dress to my means, as
you can see, but I care much more about what lies beneath
the surface than what can be seen. No matter how grotesque.
Ghastly business, judgement.

You see, me? I'll be friends with anyone.
Don't get me wrong, it's not that I wander around looking
for scary brutes and unpredictable sorts to chum around

with. No, I actually have very few friends if I'm being fully honest. So what I mean when I say, 'I'll be friends with anyone' is that anyone has the potential to be my friend no matter what disqualifying attributes others might find in them. We've all got our pasts, our demons, our . . . wee whoopsy doo da's to speak off, to pretend otherwise is to be friends with only what lies at the surface of another and that is no friend at all.

I'm one for longevity.
If you're a friend of mine, you're a friend for life, no matter how grotesque. I'm like shame, doubt and self loathing. I'll be there no matter what.

So, yes, I wouldn't ordinarily let you know of something's grotesque manner, but there are, in all areas of life, exceptions to be made, and with this door I would very much like to make one.

'Utterson! You're talking an awful lot about a door. But you've still not told us anything about it. Tell us the story, man!'

Alright, alright. Fair enough, but I just felt the need to impart upon you just how . . . unsettling that door was. OK?

Right, so it starts with a door.

The Story of the Door

It's a Sunday afternoon. Some years ago now. It's autumn. And while London does few things well, pollution and child poverty aside, my goodness, it does a good autumn.

This is a walk I take every Sunday with my old friend, Mr Enfield. A fine example of someone you probably wouldn't expect to be my friend, on account of him having a reputation for being involved in . . . well, let's say . . . a bit of this and a bit of that. You'd probably not want to be associated with someone like that. You'd probably fear for your reputation. Guilt by association, as it were. I don't mind. I'm a lawyer. And a good one. If I wrote people off I'd have no clients and then, where would I be when you needed me? Yes, I've helped Enfield out of a few sticky situations and he keeps my ear to the ground with the latest talk of the town.

It's just an ordinary Sunday, he's in his usual story mode and he's in full flow about an associate of his whose debt had caught up with him.

Enfield   So he's got John pushed right up against the wall, right, and he says, 'Alright, unless I find everything you owe me in this pocket, I'm gonna start slicing. And you're not gonna like it if I start slicing.'

Oh, I tell you he's terrified, he doesn't know whether to watch the hand heading toward his pocket or the hand that's holding the blood-stained knife up to . . . his . . . throat . . . and . . .

Utterson   We've turned the corner into a lane and he just drifts off. This is very unusual for him. To stop mid story. Normally, there could be a genuine medical emergency going on around us but if he's giving you the gory details of a triple murder or a quadruple murder he savours in the delight of bringing the story to its dramatic conclusion.

I keep expecting him to gather himself and pick things up again.

(*To* **Enfield**.) Enfield, man, what happened, did he survive? Was he sliced?

(*To audience*.) But he doesn't respond at all, he's just staring off ahead in a trance.

That's when I notice the door. It's what he's looking at. What seems to have arrested his attention. I'm struck straight away by just how unsettling it is. I'm about to point this out to Enfield when he finally pipes up:

Enfield   Utterson, have I ever told you about that door before?

Utterson   And I say:

'No.'
Because he hadn't.

And before I get a chance to ask why, he turns cold.

Enfield   Well then,

Let me tell you.

Now, I've seen a fair few things in my time, as well you know. But I have never seen anything like what I am about to tell you now.

A short while back, while I'm out and about late one night doing . . . well, never you mind, that's between me, the devil and the door man at Debenhams. Anyway, I'm walking home down this very lane and there was this . . . incident.

This horrifying incident.

It's dark. That night.

The kind of dark that has you instinctively reaching out for your mother's hand even though you know it isn't there.

It's primal.
But more than dark, it's quiet.
Really quiet.
The kind of quiet you can hear. The kind that puts your ear on high alert, searching for the slightest sound to reassure you that you still walk amongst the living. There's not a rat to be heard among the bins, not a whistle to be heard on the wind.

Then, there's footsteps. Two pairs. The first are light and fast. They're fleeing. The second – heavy and unforgiving. You can hear from where I am that they are heading toward each other but neither of them seem to realise.

The first pair, they belong to a young girl, eight years old, maybe? She's frail. Malnourished.

She's running. Sprinting. With all she's got in her weak, frail body.

And the second pair, they belong to this strange wee fella. Well . . . wee, yes, but with a fair bulk to him. And he is fair stomping down the lane at a ferocious pace.

He's charging. That's how you'd put it. He is charging down the adjacent street to this little girl.

They are unknowingly headed toward each other.
It's like it can't be stopped.

Accidents happen all the time. You know that. Big, small, the kind that ruin lives. The kind that mean folks like me need folks like you to get away with.
And this does appear to be an accident.

At first.

It's not a big bump. Nothing to write home about. I'm expecting him to get up. Dust himself off and check the child is alright then carry on.
But . . .

Utterson   He turns cold. Leans in. Close. Real close. So the space between us was nothing but shared, shallow breath. And then he comes closer still.

Enfield   Not him.

Utterson (*to* **Enfield**)   You don't mean to say he just carries on?

Enfield   Oh how I wish he'd just carried on.

Utterson (*to audience*)   He stops talking for a moment, like he's worried to tell me any more for fear it would upset me too much.

(*To* **Enfield**.) Come on man, I've heard it all before, what happened?

Enfield   Well . . . not only does he not seem to care . . .
He then, with maximum ferocity, and without even seeming to break his stride, he brings his foot down with six, powerful crashing stamps . . . and charges over her helpless body.
The sound of shattering bones fills the air.
Blood pours from her.
Before I've realised what I'm doing I'm running after him, calling:
'*Here! YOU! Get back here, right now!*'
The girl's family have rushed over to him now. Seething with rage. Baying for blood. Screaming and shouting, 'How could you . . .' this and 'What kind of a person' that.
But he's calm.
He's controlled. There's no panic. He's completely unfazed.
He turns round to see what all the fuss is about, with the air of someone who has just been asked for directions to the nearest library.
From under the brim of his hat he says he'd very much like to avoid a scene and tells them to name their price.

But the girl's dad, or maybe a scary uncle, puffs out his chest and bold as brass, goes:

'Hundred pounds.'

And I'm thinking, 'Mate. There's no way you're getting that.'

But sure enough the wee bulky lookin' fella agrees, tells them to wait a minute and with something between a grimace and a grunt, he stomps
off down the lane, into *that* door . . .

THAT DOOR, and returns with ten pounds in gold and the rest in the form of a cheque. The family then march him down to the bank – wait for it to open and for the cheque to clear, before . . . before they let him go.

Utterson   And that should have been the end of it. That there was a nasty but wealthy man living behind that grotesque door who Enfield once saw extorted to the tune of one hundred pounds after he trampled a helpless girl. And, I'll be honest, because I don't see the point in being anything else, at this point, I'm thinking 'The girl survived, I'd have told him to keep his hand in his pocket and I'd have seen him to a fair trial.'

Enfield   But it's so far from the worst part, Utterson. As horrible as it was.
The whole scene falls into near insignificance, when in the early light of the next morning, after the bank transaction is complete, I see
   His
      Face.
It's not that he is ugly, as ugly as he is, monstrous even, that's not it, there's a cup of tea and a biscuit at my door for all god's creatures. No, it's not his face. It's the look. The look he gives it's . . . it's . . . I can barely find the words to . . . Demonic? Evil? I know, I know, these words are hyperbolic but they're all I have.
The look he gave, swiftly brought out in me a sweat so strong it was like I'd run a marathon in the blink of an eye.

I must say that . . . and I know . . . hyperbole . . . but within this gaze lies the devil himself.

Utterson   And there you go, the devil. Usually, Enfield's tales are much more relatable, grounded, no matter how wild the characters are in them.
But he looks at me. He's deadly serious.

(*To* **Enfield**.) OK. Perhaps I've come across this bulky fella before. What's his name?

Enfield   Oh, if you'd met him you'd know.

Utterson   Try me. I would be keen to know If I've met the devil himself.

Enfield   OK. A Mr Hyde.

Utterson   Fuck off! HYDE?! You're quite sure the name was Hyde?

Enfield   Indeed. A Mr Edward Hyde.
So . . . you know him?

Utterson (*to audience*)   I leave it at that, thank him for his company and his story and I head toward home in a daze.

A slight shift.

He could have said any other name in the world and I'd have enjoyed his story of this 'devil man'. But not Hyde. You see, I have this friend, a Dr Jekyll. I . . . *Had* this friend? Well, it is what it is. Either way. I look after Dr Jekyll's estate. As I do with lots of my friends. Jekyll's was all fairly straightforward stuff, some left to his friends and relations, some to his alma mater, a fair chunk left to a dogs' trust, one hundred pounds to a guy called 'Big Frank' and the rest to various charitable organisations. Boiler plate stuff. But then a few years back, completely out of the blue, he changes his entire will and decrees that the whole lot be left to just one man.

Hyde.

Now, I don't make it my business to get involved in people's decisions, much like with unsolicited advice on what people should do with their hair, it's never something people thank you for.

But when people make sudden big changes to their will, I like to make sure that nothing foul is at play.

I had a client once change his will suddenly to leave his house to a sea captain. After some prodding I discovered that he lost it, along with one of his thumbs, in a poker game. Now, because I'm good at what I do, I was able to get the bet thrown out in court, the captain sent down for grievous bodily harm and force the judge to compensate my client for damages to his thumb. It pays to talk to me. I help my friends. Yes, for a fee, but I don't see why that's . . .

I wanted to do the same for Jekyll.

But any time I broached the subject of his will or this Mr Hyde, he would shut it down very quickly. This was not like Jekyll. Of all my friends we went back the furthest. We could and would share our deepest and darkest. But not since Hyde appeared.

The whole thing was bad enough when Hyde was just a name in a will – but now that I knew him to be a child trampling monster . . . it was torture.

The Search For Mr Hyde

Utterson   I get the urge to visit, who I knew to be my oldest mutual friend of Dr Jekyll, a Dr Lanyon, in the hope that he could shed some light.
Wishful thinking.

Lanyon   Jekyll? My goodness me. You come here and you talk of Jekyll?
Don't you speak his name in my house. That man owes me at least one apology. And a Persian rug.
No, I've not seen him in many a moon. Years in fact. Three-and-a-half years to be more accurate. If you require more precision than that then you'll have to bear with me while I consult my journal. But should my estimations suffice then listen up and I'll tell you for why it has been so long.
He became too . . . let's say . . . fanciful . . . for me. Now, look around this gaff and you'll see I obviously have a penchant for the fancy, a rare knack for picking out the most delicate whimsy, for ordaining my world with extravagances of the extreme. I have, for example, drawn over these very window glasses, the finest and most outrageous silk that one can find in a ten mile radius, you just try getting fancier drapes without access to a horse. Go on! You can't. You just can't!
And so yes, I love the fanciful. But I am also, as you know, a man of science, and when it comes to science I have no room for the fanciful. There is simply no room for fanciful ideas in the scientific sphere. Of course we need the big thinkers, we need the dreamers, those who believe the great unanswered questions can be answered, that there are mysteries yet to be solved, that there are discoveries yet to be discovered. We do. We need them. These . . . renegades. But I dare say, with Jekyll, and do please forgive me for speaking ill of your friend, the man has gone absolutely and quite irreversibly off his barnett. Wrong in the head, sir. Indulging in matters of the ridiculous. He pushed beyond unfurrowed scientific ground and sought instead to advance the most worrisome of studies. The only relief is that his work is, I am confident to say, utter balderdash and so therefore can do no harm.

Utterson   OK, fair enough, I'll say no more of him. In fact, it's not actually him I'm here to talk about, I was actually wondering if you have ever come across an acquaintance of his, a Mr Hyde?

Lanyon   Now, I know, Utterson, that you'll stand by men on their way down in this world and I've yet to run the proper analysis to determine whether that is an enviable or an abhorrent trait that you hold, but I have too much work to be getting on with to get dragged down by the likes of Jekyll and the miserable company he keeps. We don't talk. I cut him clean off. For I am not a duck. Am I? Am I? Am I a duck? No, you are correct. I am not a duck. And therefore, as I am not a duck, it is only right that I do not respond to quacks.

Utterson (*to audience*)   As I say, wishful thinking. However I will testify that they really were rather exquisite looking drapes.

*

I'm usually a very good sleeper.
Something about playing my part in the justice system really helps me rest easy.
Though, of course, I have from time to time, had people, usually families of a victim of some heinous crime or other, shout to me after a trial, 'How do you sleep at night?!'
And I'd say, 'I don't know, but I always find a way.'

But that night, I lie there with images of Enfield's story and the brute that my friend Jekyll was embroiled with or indebted to has my mind racing, my heart pounding, my stomach knotted and sleep will not come.

That word evil keeps swirling round my mind. I'd have told you prior to that moment that evil doesn't exist. Only right and wrong, and even then, they're very moveable feasts in my eyes. But Enfield used the word so sincerely that it had gotten to me.
And when he applied it to Hyde.

I had to find him.
If sleep wouldn't come, sleep could wait.

I sat up in bed and said out loud to myself:
'If he be Mr Hyde then I shall be Mr Seek!'

And if there had been people around to hear it then I'm almost certain they would have laughed, because, well, what a line!
But as it was, I was alone.

I get out of bed and head straight out the door.
Then go back for my shoes.
And head straight out again into the quiet of the night. My feet taking me in the direction of the grotesque door.
Thinking perhaps I would see him there in the early hours, as Enfield had.

I do not.

I go back at the break of day.

Nothing.

At peak business hours.

Nothing.

I return again and again. At the small hours, the really small hours, the teeny toatie teensy weensy hours. In the gap between breakfast and lunch, the gap between high tea and dinner.

After weeks of this I start to wonder if perhaps Enfield has made the whole thing up. As an act of mischief or revenge. It's possible I'd told him the name Hyde back when Jekyll had changed his will and he stored it for such a time that he would want to give me a fright.

But this was wishful thinking at best.
For,

   at last . . .

a shadow

emerged.

Every bit as gruesome as I had feared. Worse even. Unfathomably so. The monstrous dark shape that it cast on the wall was so perplexing, so brutal that it felt impossible that it could be human at all.

And, well, that's because . . .

Well, it wasn't – A pigeon had simply walked past a street lamp.

But so ready was I to see the grotesque, so ready was I to play into this game of monsters, that I let this trick of the light play into my darkest fears.

I let out a nervous chuckle, as if to tell myself that I was being daft, that I should get Enfield's story out of my head, move on from all this 'evil' business and get back to reality.

But as soon as I let my guard down for that split second to laugh, to let that slip of humanity in. That very second.

He arrives.

And I'm thinking, this surely has to be another trick of the light. But it's not. It's real. The very air around me seems to run cold. It's as though all the energy of the night sky is drawn toward this source, where it is destroyed.

Every instinct I have is telling me to run. To vanish. But my feet are planted.

And though my brain is trying to summon the cowardice to flee, my mouth betrays me.

And the words

'Mr Hyde, I presume.'

Are already filling the air between me and this . . . man.

He hesitates for the briefest of moments . . . but then he is gone. Through the door. And I am alone.

I could spend all evening trying and failing to find words to describe what he made me feel in that moment. I don't think I'll ever find the words.

It's like if I were to ask you to imagine a new colour. You could try. Go on, try. You could give this new colour a name. Fujunia? Asenite? Harbeen? Plomp? Maybe you could give it a vague description. It's jovial? It's bold? It's boisterous, lively, convivial? But to actually conjure that colour in someone's mind? It's impossible. Our imagination is bound by the limits of our experience. Nothing can prepare us for the reality of something truly new. Like falling in love. We think we know it. We think we understand it. But we don't. Until we feel it. And even then, try as we may, we can't truly describe it. It must be experienced.

Look, I know, you know what I now know. But see then . . . I . . . I'd felt nothing like it before and I've felt nothing like it since.

If there is one thing I would say to try and describe him, to point at him with words that might begin to do him some justice, it's that Enfield was right. I've dealt with some bad men who've done some bad things but if ever there was Satan's signature upon a man. It was on him.

And to think that as I am stood there, stricken with fear and foreboding, all I could think was 'Poor Jekyll'.

A shift.

I feel I should say a few things to you about Jekyll.
Some things that might make sense to you and might make you think that I should have been connecting dots. Seeing the signs. That the evidence was there.

He had a bit of a wild youth.
OK?
What, you didn't?

Everyone's got shame, some skeletons in their closet. Several things they will find pretty difficult to forgive themselves for.

Well, Jekyll had a lot. Jekyll went properly off the rails a few times. Yeah, some of it was . . . wild. But I'd seen how caring he could be. He stayed with us one semester when he was trying to screw his head on and to gain some perspective. While he was there, my mother became sick. He spent so much time with her. Making her smile, holding her hand, putting a damp cloth to her head and listening to her stories over and over again. He had the patience of a saint. He waited with her until the very end. Until her very last breath. And after she died he paid for her funeral and took on the payments on her house so that I would not have to give up my studies in order to find the money. I owe everything I have to him and even though I could afford to pay him back many times over now, he'd never hear of it. He'd gotten his life back and credited me with the saving. I'd seen him make amends, make a better man of himself. He levelled out. All he asked in return was that I help keep him safe and well and on the straight and narrow.

So, when this Hyde character turned up in his will, I honestly thought he was holding my friend to ransom over the ghost of an old sin, the cancer of some concealed disgrace from his youth.

It bothered me that this monster could make such a puppet of Jekyll's conscience. For, as wild as Jekyll's past may have been to the eyes of polite society it was nothing I couldn't defend in court. Judge me all you want. I put loyalty before right or wrong. In any case, if he was compared to this Hyde, Jekyll would look a saint.

A slight shift.

I continue to perform my professional duties as best I can, but this man consumes my every other thought. He has invaded the space in my mind I would ordinarily reserve for relaxation or ruminating on some future pleasures – an upcoming chess game with a fierce opponent, a fine gin being imported to my house from Holland, yes, Holland, not only did the Dutch invent gin, they perfected it, and if anyone tries to tell you that either of those claims belong to England you can be sure to write them off as nothing more than a fool or a dull patriot. With this space consumed at all times with thoughts of Hyde, I become unable to rest or unwind.

I attempt to settle myself by building a case on Hyde. Try to find something concrete I could take to Jekyll that would show him what kind of a monster he'd become involved with in the hope that he would open up to me and let me help him. Or, better still, I could get Hyde locked up somewhere, preferably for life, where Jekyll would be safe from him. But I find nothing. Not a thing. Apart from a chequing account he held at the bank but no one working there had any memory of him. There are no school records, no health records, no sign of him ever having had a past at all.

I have found in my work that those with no past to speak of often have the most to hide.

Nothing else for it. I must speak to Jekyll.

And, as fate would have it, I soon receive an invite to his house for one of his legendarily lavish dinner parties.

He hasn't thrown one for years but they are back with a bang. No expense spared and all the very best of stuff. The night seems to be some attempt to reach back out to his old scientific buddies from whom he'd drifted. I can't quite see how I make the list? Conversational buffer? Eye witness? The evening is as intense as it is opulent. This is in no small part due to the presence of Lanyon who proves, it would seem, that not even the greatest of moral or scientific concerns are ever quite enough to keep a man and his stomach away from the finest cheese and wine going gratis.

Lanyon   You are a charlatan! . . .

Utterson   He says, in the middle of a deep philosophical debate about the moral boundaries of science.

Lanyon   . . . A charlatan and rogue. A rogue. And a monster! You'll be the end of us all. Not just the scientific community but life as we know it. Sure you throw a nice party. And the cheese? The cheese is exquisite but you'll be the end of us all!

Utterson   Jekyll, though, he is calm, he is controlled, he is completely unfazed in the face of all of this. He is light and airy. Quiet, humble, confident. There is a real breeziness to him. He doesn't even seem to falter in his serenity when Lanyon brings his mother into it. Something Lanyon would do from time to time.
Jekyll speaks well, tells him he is as welcome to his opinions as he is the cheese, but that we cannot live in a world where we halt the search for knowledge merely to settle the anxieties of Lanyon, or anyone else for that matter. That science owes nothing to worry . . . and that we must continue to make discoveries. *Then* make sense of them. Whatever the consequences.

Seeing him like this almost makes me forget my worries. This is a man who's wild and tempered days are long behind him and he certainly does not seem like a man tortured by any guilty conscious or blackmail.
But Lanyon, as if to jolt me out of my momentary comfort, yells:

Lanyon   If you mess with the darker side of science, if you dig too deep into the unknown, Jekyll, you will regret it. You will! YOU WILL!

Utterson   That word hangs in the air long enough for me to know it would be remiss of me to go home without raising the subject with him.

I just need to wait until everyone else has gone.

Now, I'm often last to leave a party. I've been told by many hosts over the years that they like to detain me for my dry company when the light-hearted and the loose-tongued have departed. Apparently my 'rich silences' help them prepare for the upcoming solitude while they sober their mind after the expense and strain of all the gaiety. So Jekyll would never suspect anything by my staying.

Just wait it out. Easy, right? Well, no, it's far from easy. Largely because Lanyon, who is now just muttering obscenities and slander under his breath, seems to be going nowhere until either the cheese is finished or he has a heart attack.

When Lanyon eventually gets up to visit the bathroom, I seize the opportunity to gather up the remains of the spread. I bundle the whole lot, tablecloth and all, and with one swift flick of the wrist, I launch the lot out the window, into the street below like a care package for the rats.

You can see the relief on Jekyll's face when Lanyon returns, sees the food has gone, wipes the crumbs from his lapels, gives the host a grunt and a nod, and stumbles out into the night like a badger that'd just given blood.

(*To* **Jekyll**.) Jekyll, you know this will of yours /

Jekyll   / Oh, Utterson. I have never met anyone as obsessed and distressed about anything in this world as you are about my will. Well perhaps that inflexible pedant Lanyon when it comes to my work.

Utterson   You know I never approved of it.

Jekyll   Yes, I know. You *have* told me this on several occasions.

Utterson   OK. Well then. Allow me to tell you again. Please! Just . . . hear me out.
When we discussed these things in the past, all I had was this bad feeling . . . But that was before. That was when I knew nothing of this Hyde. The things I have heard, Jekyll dear friend, are simply abominable. Whatever it is that's going on here. I can get you out of it. You can trust me.

Jekyll   I do trust you.
If it were needed, I would entrust my life to you.

But right now I want you to trust me.
It is all in my control. Not his. Honestly.
My bond with him is completely and utterly my own doing.
Whenever I say so, he is gone. I hold that power in my hand.
Now, I hope that some day soon we can stop talking about my bloody will!
But before that, I want you to make me a promise. A promise that no matter what, you will deliver what is Hyde's by right. That you will help him.

Utterson (*to audience*)   And then he puts his hand on my arm, gently, and says:

Jekyll   If you knew the whole story, the whole strange situation, you would help him.

Utterson (*to audience*)   I let out a sigh that seems longer than my lungs are capable of. Hopelessly buying time waiting for divine inspiration. But nothing comes.

(*To* **Jekyll**.) Ok then, I promise.

Heads home.

The Carew Murder Case

Utterson   Over the next few months I am able to suppress my urge to talk about him and seeing as no one else mentions his name to me, I'm slowly able to think about him less and less. But he never fully leaves my thoughts. He's always in there. Somewhere.

I settle down for a quiet drink by the fire and a memory of Hyde rushes to the front of my thinking, bringing me out in a cold sweat. Someone taps my shoulder in a busy market and I cower into a ball at the sudden memory of his presence, panicked that he had returned. Whenever I relax or let my guard down, he is there, ready to pounce into my thoughts and render me terrified.

People say that fear is nothing more than an inconvenient weakness of the human spirit.

Well I don't.

I think it's a biological superpower. It keeps us on our toes. It stops us from sharing our houses with tigers. Without fear we'd never survive. It reminds us that no matter how quiet it gets, the threat is still out there.

And Hyde was still very much out there. And before long he would come bursting right back into my life.

*

It's a calm foggy morning, some months later. I'm sitting having breakfast when I get a call from the police asking me to come and identify a body, or rather, what was left of a body. The man had been carrying a letter addressed to me when he was attacked.
And I'm warned that, even though I've seen a fair few dead bodies in my time, the sight of this man's corpse has turned the stomach of the toughest coppers in the station – and so – I should be prepared for 'a hell of a sight'.

I tell them not to worry and that I'd be there as soon as I'm finished my breakfast. And if that seems heartless to you, I will share with you the best advice that I was given to me by my mother:

'If you think you're going to be sick, make sure you've something to bring up.'

And I am so glad I have something to bring up because the sight of him would instantly sober even the drunkest of sailors.

His face is nothing but a trampled mush of red and purple mixed with shards of bone and hair. The stuff of actual nightmares.

I swear to god if not for the birth mark on his right wrist there would be no way of identifying him.
I confirm that the victim is . . . was my client, Sir Danvers Carew MP. They are happy with this as it matches the signature on the letter addressed to me.

The officer says aloud, to all and no one: 'In all my days I aint ever seen anything so unholy.'

Another officer is taking a statement from an eye witness who is still shaking from what she saw unfold from her first floor window.

Witness   It was a perfect evening. Just perfect. I was sat at the window, looking out, thinking about just how . . . perfect it was. A man walked into view. A perfect little addition to the scene. Just a perfect oil painting of an evening.
Then another man arrives and pulls beauty and hope from the air quicker than summer turns to winter in Aberdeen. Wielding his cane like a madman he flies into a rage. The nice man backs off but this only gives the monster enough room to swing and with an ape like fury, he rains blows of his cane down on the man's head like the crashing of a thousand waves.

And he does not stop until he is quite content that the man was dead.

Utterson   The officer thanks the witness and says he will now approach every resident in the area in the search for information. But I know, in the pit of my stomach, that there was only one soul I have ever crossed paths with that I could even suspect of having the capacity to perform such an act of depravity.

And as if to confirm my suspicions, the officer shows me the remains of the cane used to beat Danvers Carew, which had been abandoned at the scene. This shocks me for two reasons: One, I had gifted this cane to Jekyll years ago. And two, I knew the wood to be hickory, one of the strongest in nature. The force that must have been used to shatter the thing is unfathomable.

I think for a moment of my promise to Jekyll but the weight of that wood in my hand tells me all I need to know.

(*To the* **Copper**.) Officer, I am most certain that this is the work of a Mr Edward Hyde.

Copper   Can you think of anywhere this Hyde could be? Do you know of any associates of his?

Sound – a distant ringing.

Utterson (*to audience*)   I take a long hard think . . . . . 'No.'

I go straight to see Jekyll.

(*To* **Jekyll**.) Jekyll, have you heard the news?

Jekyll   Yes. Awful business. Just awful. Carew was a good man. He didn't deserve that. He didn't deserve that at all. It's awful.

Utterson   News travels fast, I've only just now come from identifying the body.
You must know that Hyde is responsible for this hideous attack. The police have evidence and they will hunt for him.

Now, I've managed to keep your name out of it but you have to promise me that you'll cut off all ties with him immediately.

Jekyll   I swear to god, I'm done with him. It is all at an end. I swear. People are safe from him. Please don't ask how I know – but he's gone. I swear.

Utterson (*to audience*)   I feel he's over selling it . . .

Jekyll   I have proof, he has written me a letter. You just have to trust me.

Utterson   He hands me this scrap of paper, written in an odd, upright hand and signed by Edward Hyde. It more or less says that he will be eternally grateful for Jekyll's many generosities and that he is truly sorry to have let him down and for never paying him back but the time has come for him to leave and never return and that no one should worry for his safety.

(*To* **Jekyll**.) Do you have the envelope?'

Jekyll   No. I . . . must have . . . emptied my waste basket into the fire earlier. Terrible habit, I know, but I do love the extra kick of heat if gives with it burns bright and fast for that moment.

Utterson   One more thing before I go. Hyde forced you to change your will, didn't he?

(*To audience*.) He looks embarrassed, regretful and a little faint. Then he shuts his mouth tight and nods.

Honestly I was so proud of myself. Thought I'd fuckin' cracked it.

(*To* **Jekyll**.) Well you're quite safe now. You have had a lucky escape.

(*To audience*.) As I leave, I stop to speak to Jekyll's butler, Poole. I let him know that it would be wise for him to remember all that Jekyll has done for him over the years and to stay very quiet about this morning's visitor with the letter, but to my surprise:

Poole   There have been no letters here today, sir.

Utterson   That's very good, Poole, you are wise indeed.

Poole   No sir, I honestly don't follow you. There have been no letters here today. Just the newspapers and they ain't worth a shilling of shit 'cause they ain't got nothing in them about the murder. That'll be in the late edition I should hope. Out soon.

Utterson   How odd, you're sure there's nothing you're forgetting. Nothing dropped in by . . . Mr Hyde?

Poole   Good god, no.

Utterson   Thank you, Poole.

The Remarkable Incident of Dr Lanyon

With Sir Danvers Carew MP being such a beloved member of society, his murder is the talk of the city. From parliament bars to the poorhouse yards, everyone is talking about the monstrous killer that is still on the loose, each with their own theory as to where he could be.

Some say he was living at the top of big Ben where he was scoping out his next victim. Some say he was hiding in the underground tunnels. Others said he'd 'gone up to Scotland where he could blend in with the hideous locals'.

And once the police put out the announcement that there's now a large bounty on the killer's head – well there are soon more rumors as to his whereabouts than there are eels in the Thames.

With Hyde gone, Jekyll really starts to flourish. He invests himself deeply in his charity work (which he has been neglecting of late) and is hosting parties again. He and Lanyon even seem to bury the hatchet – but only after Jekyll concedes to having lost his way scientifically.

I'm round at Jekyll's regularly, having a great night each time.
All is well.
But then one night, Poole denies me entry to see Jekyll.

Poole   The master is confined to the house and seeing no one.

Utterson (*to audience*)   I don't think too much of it. At first. Everyone is entitled to a night in alone if they want it.
But then, every time I return after that, it's the same.

Poole   Confined to the house.

Remaining in his room tonight.

Unable to entertain at present.

Please sir, Dr Jekyll would like some space.

Utterson   I pay Lanyon a visit, to see if he could shed any light on Jekyll's sudden turn for the reclusive. But he does not put me at ease. At all. Quite the opposite.

He is an absolute shell of a man. The life and spark has gone from his eye. His very soul seems to have left his limp, frail frame.
I approach him in shock and caution but he just stares past me in soft focus making no adjustment to meet my gaze or register my presence.

(*To* **Lanyon**.) Jesus, Lanyon, what in god's name is the matter with you? You look like you've been chased out of hell by Satan's rottweiler.

Lanyon   I have had a fright. An almighty fright. A soul-shaking rattle to my core from which I will never recover.

Utterson (*to audience*)   And I say, 'Jekyll is quite ill as well, sir. Might you have the same thing?'

But then at the mere mention of Jekyll's name he shifts from frail to terrified. He cowers back and feebly raises his hands over his as if to protect himself from harm.

Lanyon   You take that man's name out your mouth while you are in my house. You speak not of him. I never want to hear his name again.

Utterson (*to* **Lanyon**)   Whatever is the matter?

Lanyon   He lied. He said he'd seen the error of his ways. But he lies. He said he was done with his journey into the dark side. But he lies. He is the devil himself. I told you he would be the end of us all. Now, leave me here to die in what little dignity I have left.

Utterson   Lanyon, whatever has happened, you'll be alright. I assure you. Folk have seen and heard as bad and worse, I assure you, and every one of them made it out to make sense of it on a clearer day. All will be well. No one ever died of shock.

(*To audience*.) But . . . he's dead in a fortnight. Stopped eating. Stopped drinking.
Like a bird that knows that it's time to go, he found himself a quiet place to die and off he went.

Well, there you go.

*

Jekyll makes no appearance at the funeral.

But I need him to tell me what the hell happened. Poole denies me access again so I write a strongly worded letter and leave it with him and head home to my favoured chair, my stress-chair, where I intend I sit and stew for a good while.

But I'm barely in my seat an hour, hardly enough time to even build up a good anger sweat, and Poole is at the door, straight from Jekyll's house with a response.

Firstly he says he doesn't blame himself for Lanyon's 'demise' but that Lanyon was probably 'right to avoid him'. He then goes on to say that he now wishes to 'henceforth live a life of extreme seclusion'. He tells me 'not to worry, or doubt our friendship', that he has brought on himself a 'terrible punishment and a danger that I cannot name'.

He closes by saying he is the 'chief of sinners' but that he is the 'chief of sufferers also' and that he never thought 'the earth capable of containing such sufferings and terrors' as he has brought to it.

The one thing I can do, he says, the *one thing* I can do to 'lighten this insufferable situation' was to . . . respect his silence.

But you see, here's the thing. I've already got *two* dead friends. One from actual shock and one from a beating so bad they had to pour him into his coffin, and I am genuinely panicked that he will be next – so I'm hardly just going to leave him alone.

And then I noticed the P.S. asking me to reinstate Mr Edward Hyde as the sole beneficiary of his will!

In the Lane

The next day I find myself, once again compelled to go stand by that door. That grotesque door.

And then I notice, in the gutter of the lane, the scrapped remains of Jekyll's table cloth that I had launched from the window earlier . . .

And it suddenly dawns on me that this door connects to Jekyll's property . . . such is the maze like structure of these lanes!

I head to the front of the building.

I approach with caution, looking for movement at the windows:

(*Shouts.*) Jekyll, is that you?

A figure moves in my direction but comes no closer.

(*Calls to* **Jekyll**.) Jekyll. It's me. Utterson. I'm worried for you my friend. Whatever it is, I can help you old friend. Won't you please talk with me a moment.

(*To audience.*) The figure moves slowly forward until nearly up at the glass. And I can almost make out . . . Jekyll's face . . . but he's cowering away as though the low winter sun is burning him.

(*To* **Jekyll**.) Jekyll. It's me. It's Utterson. Come, man, being outside would do you the world of good. Go get your coat and let's take a walk together.

(*To audience.*) He takes some time to answer and seems to be struggling a great deal . . .

Jekyll   It's very good to see you. But no, no, no, it is impossible. Please don't mistake me. I am very glad to see you Utterson. It really is a great pleasure. But no, I shan't be leaving here. And I would have you in but that's not possible either.

Utterson (*to* **Jekyll**)   Well then, don't you worry, that's quite alright. It's good to see you in any case, why don't we just chat from where we are. That'll more than do.

(*To audience*.) And with great relief he smiles and says:

Jekyll   Very good.

Utterson   But almost as soon as the words have left his mouth, his entire being seems to shift, the smile is stricken from his face and replaced by an expression of such abject terror and despair that my blood is frozen cold.

I walk away in stunned silence.

'God forgive us. God forgive us all.'

The Last Night

I can't tell you the route I take to get home or how long it takes me. I remember nothing. But I was snapped back to reality when the door bell rings and I find Poole on my door step. He is visibly shaken. I am dealing with a desperate man, for sure.

(*To* **Poole**.) OK Poole, come in and take a seat while I pour you a drink. Now, take a moment and try to tell me as exactly as you can, what is the matter?

(*To audience*.) He sits trembling for a moment, he doesn't even consider drinking the gin in his hand, he just stares at the motion of the liquid in the glass – which does seem to steady his focus and calm him down to just a frenzy.

Poole   You know the doctor's ways of late, sir, and how he has shut himself away. Well, I'm afraid, sir that . . . that . . .

Utterson   Poole, try to be explicit. What are you afraid of?

Poole   I've been afraid for weeks now, sir, but . . . but . . . but . . .

Utterson (*to audience*)   Now, I don't like taking a sharp tone with the vulnerable, but I needed clarity.

(*To* **Poole**.) Come on man! Something has driven you here tonight? Now, for god's sake, tell me what it is!

(*To audience*.) He slowly turns his gaze from his glass to me.

Poole   Well I . . . I fear he is not alone. I fear he has someone . . . or something . . . in there with him.

Utterson   Have you told anyone else?

Poole   No sir, only you

Utterson   Good man.

(*To audience*.) I grab my coat, skull my gin for dutch courage and to be sure of it, I skull his as well.

We take to the street.

The night is of biblical proportions. The wild and eerie bitter-cold wind brings the blood to our faces and keeps the words out of our mouths.

We arrive at that door. Listen closely over the pounding of my heart.

From the other side I hear what sounds like scurrying.

Despite the cold, Poole is so scared he has broken outing a terrible sweat

He leans in close to the door, takes a deep breath and gives it a very gentle tap.

Poole   Dr Jekyll, sir, it is Poole, I have Mr Utterson here to see you.

Utterson   The scurrying comes to a sudden stop. Followed by a silence.

Then very faintly, someone from beyond the door attempts to talk. But barely is there a word out before the voice is interrupted by a hideous growl.

There's another brief silence . . .

Before a voice that is broken and haunting:

Jekyll   Tell him I cannot be seen!

Poole   By the light and love of all that is holy – that is NOT Jekyll. *That* is HYDE!

Jekyll is in danger!

Utterson (*to* **Poole**)   'Poole, fetch me an axe. Jekyll is in danger!'

The rest of London is humming solemnly. People sleep. Last orders are supped. Street lamps glow. People stagger home in the fog.

But I stand in this grotesque lane . . . Listening to the weeping. The hollering, howling weep of a tortured soul.

I lift the axe. The light bounces off its sharp edge in such a way that it almost makes a *sschiing* noise in my brain.

Adrenaline. Dopamine. Norepinephrine. All coursing through my body.

There is another call from behind the door.

Jekyll   Utterson! For god's sake, have mercy!

Utterson (*to* **Jekyll**)   I say . . .!

Down with the door!!!

(*To audience.*) I bring the axe down on the door with a tremendous, satisfying force.

And again.

We throw caution to the wind and go at it hell for leather. I swing the axe down as Poole rams the door with his shoulders in alternating blows.
Light breaks through the panels.

Jekyll   Please, Utterson, the last thing I ask is that you try to remember me as you did before.

Utterson   And with one final, hefty kick, the lock bursts in sunder and the door falls inwards on the carpet.

I clutch the axe firm in both hands as we burst in.

But there is no rushing toward us. No violent scene.

I see nothing but the most ordinary scene.

And there in the middle of the room is . . . Hyde. Or . . . Now, I know you know. I know . . . We all already know. But there. Then. In the shadows, I . . .

(*To* **Jekyll**.) Hyde. What have you done with Dr Jekyll?

(*To audience.*) He turns to face me.

Then, just for a split second, he . . . twitches? Hollers?
Howls? Cries? Sobs? . . . Begs? . . . Whimpers?

He looks me in the eye.

His eyes.

In those eyes, my dear friend . . . Henry Jekyll.

I look at him there and see him. Pure Jekyll.

You see, people think there's potions in stories like this. That
there's magic and transformations. But there isn't. That's
just something we tell ourselves. To help us hide from the
fact that monsters are just people. And sometimes they are
people we know. If there's potions and magic, it's easier to
tell ourselves we couldn't have seen it coming. When we
probably should have. And quite possibly even did. But
maybe we choose not to see it. So we can avoid the truth. So
we can deny it. To help us make sense of it all. To protect a
friend. To protect ourselves.

He leans in. Takes a deep, meaningful breath and he tells
me, in no uncertain terms.

Jekyll   I'm here . . .
I am Hyde. I created him.
Utterson . . . I released him from inside myself.

You know me. You know I have fought my whole life to
suppress my dark side. But with Hyde, I have been free to
act upon my base impulses. Free to act without consequence.
Danvers Carew, that was me.
Lanyon. Me.
That girl in the lane. Me.
Countless other stories that you've heard (and many more
that you haven't). All true. All me.
Me.
Me.
Me.
Oh and I loved it. All of it. The entire, horrible business.

Somewhere deep down, you have always known.
All these years you've known what I'm capable of . . .
The good and the bad.

You could have taken me in. Several times. But you didn't.
You could have found me. Brought me to a stop. But you
didn't.

And that's your Hyde, Utterson. That's your monster.
Helping bad men run free.
Isn't it?

Utterson   I don't know what you want me to tell you. That
I told him no? That he had me all wrong? That I cared for
fairness and I'd fairly see him put away?

That I fought for justice?

Poole, who, having listened to all this and was by nature
compelled to do the 'right thing' pipes up saying that we
should go. That we should go and call for help.

'The right thing.'

I didn't want him to come to any harm. I didn't. I really
didn't.

But then . . .

I know what will happen if I let him leave.
So I tell him, 'I'll . . . I'll go check outside for help.'

Leaving them both alone, leaving the axe . . . leaving it in my
control

I walk out.

One last job for Hyde.

I told you. I'm not the good guy.

Ends.

Printed in the USA
CPSIA information can be obtained
at www.ICGtesting.com
LVHW020947171024
794056LV00003B/1005